# The Stories
# and Lessons
# Behind the Sermons

*BY:*

*Apostle Vincent J. Gilchrist*

*Eagles Word Christian Publisher, LLC*
New York

## Psalm 34:8 (CEV)

"Discover for yourself  that the Lord is kind. Come to him for protection, and you will be glad.!"

# Acknowledgements

Thank you, Lord, for the gift you have given me and for choosing me to represent you through your Word. I submit myself humbly to you God. Please continue to use me to spread your good news to the world.

To my family whom I love very much, all of you are a special part of my life. I am blessed to have you all on my journey.

To my Pastor and Godfather – Apostle Levar A. Williams, I thank you for taking the time to encourage me when I need it most.

To my Godfather - Apostle Alfred L. Phillips, thank you for praying for me and for always being willing to help me whenever, and for whatever, I need you for.

Special thank you to my Godmother – Mother Alice Goodson. I want you to know that you are very special to me. Thank you for your love, prayers, and concern for me. I want you to know how much I appreciate and treasure you. **Proverbs 31:31 (CEV)** says "Show her respect – praise her in public for what she has done."

# Introduction

This book contains small messages that I have preached over the years, and a few of the stories behind those messages. Herein are some of those sermons that I want to introduce. I pray that you enjoy reading them as much as I enjoyed preaching them.

### 1 Corinthians 9:16 CEV)

"I don't have any reason to brag about preaching the good news. Preaching is something God told me to do, and if I don't do it, I am doomed."

### Jeremiah 1:9 (CEV)

"The Lord reached out his hand, then he touched my mouth and said, "I am giving you the words to say,"

# Table of Contents

# Do Not Quit

*March 20, 1992*
*(7:00 PM)*

Friday night at 309 Tompkins Avenue – at the time this was the location of the New Covenant House of Prayer, where the late Evangelist Shirley Davis was Pastor. Pastor Davis had reached out to me and asked if I would preach for her. I told her that I would be honored to fulfill that request. I preached a sermon titled "Whatever you do, do not quit." This sermon has been a blessing from the day that I preached it, until now. Many have been blessed by it – including myself.

# 2

## The Power of a Testimony

*December 17, 1994*
*Saturday night*

I remember back in 1983, the late Pastor Timothy Wright recorded an album entitled "Testify". I had it on cassette tape, and I wore out the cassette and broke it because I kept rewinding and playing that song (testify) so often. I fell in love with that song! Back in those days in church, during the devotional service, the deacon would ask if anyone had a testimony. I enjoyed hearing the people get up one by one and testify about what God had done for them and how good He is. I too would testify to the goodness of the Lord. In today's services there is no more testimony time. It has been replaced by praise and worship.

I thank God for imparting this sermon in my spirit to share with His people on this Saturday night in 1994.

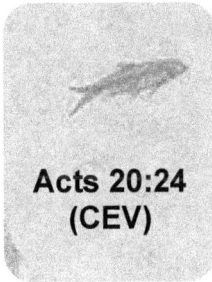

**Acts 20:24 (CEV)**

"But I don't care what happens to me, as long as I finish the work the Lord Jesus gave me to do. And this work is to tell the good news about God's gift of undeserved grace."

## God's Grace

When I was a young child, I recall my mother having an old song/hymn book. Looking through it one day I came upon a wonderful song entitled "Amazing Grace". We sang it at church also, and now that I am an adult I still love to sing this song. It has become one of my favorite songs.

*November 17, 2007*
*Saturday*

This sermon stresses how God's grace is covering us like a blanket and protecting us, even in times when we do not realize that we need covering. Let the truth of it permeate your heart and mind so that you can become an expression of His love, kindness, and goodness to others.

Our Heavenly Father is not selfish, and He holds nothing from us. He lavishly pours out His grace upon us. Instead of merely digesting small bites of His Word and short visits in His presence on Sundays, we ought to devour whole "meals" each day and feed your soul. Follow the advice from the Psalms: "open wide so you can taste and see that the Lord is good." (Psalm 81:10; 34:8).

## An Urgent Prayer

*September 28, 2003*
*Sunday Night*

One morning at 2:00 AM, Pastor Gloria E. Knight called me because she was not feeling well, and she asked me to pray for her/with her. When I finished praying, I read two scriptures to her – **Psalm 120:1 (The Message)** "I'm in trouble. I cry to God, desperate for an answer", and **2 Corinthians 4:8-9 (TLB)** "We are pressed on every side by troubles, but not crushed and broken".

We become perplexed because we do not understand why things happen the way they do, but we should not give up, or quit. We may feel chased down or pursued, but God is there for us. We may get knocked down, but we get up again and continue moving. I thank God for this sermon that lets us know that some situations and circumstances in our lives appear desperate, and our pain might be deep. In these times you may only be able to muster up a 911/SOS prayer to God, using the words: "God, I need help"! God hears them all. He knows our names, and all about the situations that we find ourselves in. Like a Heavenly dispatcher, He sends exactly what is needed – including any advice that is required to help us through the crisis. Keep a listening ear and remember that help will be on the way.

◇ **5** ◇

# The Frailty of Life

*April 13, 2012*
*Friday (Noonday prayer, by phone)*

While on my B65 bus commute heading downtown, I received a text message from the mother of my two godsons that read "life is so fragile. Please handle it with tender, loving, care". This message is true, and it made my day – it came at the right time, and it was something I absolutely needed to read! Two scriptures came to my mind –

- **Psalm 90:12 (CEV)**

"Teach us to use wisely all the time we have."

- **James 4:14 (CEV)**

"What do you know about tomorrow? How can you be so sure about your life? It is nothing more than mist that appears for only a little while before it disappears."

This sermon that I preached says that it is not a good idea to cruise through life thinking that we are invincible, and that everything is going to be alright (only to discover that we are much more fragile than we thought). It only takes one phone call from the doctor telling us that we have a life-threatening disease, or the swerve of a careless driver in front of us, to make us aware that life is uncertain. The Lord reminds us that our lives are fragile – like a vapor or fog. We do not know how long we have here on earth, and we certainly do not know what tomorrow may bring.

There are no guarantees! None of us are assured that we have another breath. The Psalmist has an important piece of advice/warning in Psalm 90:12. Let us choose to live life as though it were our last time on earth by being more  loving, more forgiving, generously giving, and speaking kindly.

My friends, that is how to handle life with tender, loving, care.

$$\diamond\ 6\ \diamond$$

## Never Stop Praising

*December 31, 2007*
*Monday (New Years Eve)*

I recall one night on my way to church, while standing at the bus stop waiting for the B15 bus to come, a lady drove up in her BMW, parked, got out, and walked up to me. She then stated to me "Mister, God is so good to me. I just want to give him praise and share my testimony with you". After she shared all  of what she wanted to tell me, she said to me "never stop praising God!". She returned to her car and drove off. All I could say in that moment was "thank you Jesus, this is my message for tonight!".

I thank God for giving me this sermon to preach because He sent His messenger in a way that there was no doubt about what He wanted me to say. I say to you all, let us continue to praise God anyhow. This is where your help will come from.

## ⟨ 7 ⟩

## Spontaneous Praise

*July 12, 2009*
*Sunday Night*

There is a wonderful song that says, "I don't know what you've come to do, but I come to clap my hands, I've come to stomp my feet; surely didn't come to look at you, but I've come to praise the Lord." Yet another song says, " I love to praise Him, I love to praise His holy name."

### Psalm 100:2 (CEV)

"Be joyful and sing as you come in to worship the Lord!"

### Psalm 100:4 (CEV)

"Be thankful and praise the Lord as you enter his temple."

This is what we must do when we come together in the house of the Lord to worship.

I was on the corner of Dean Street and Rochester Avenue at 4:00 PM waiting for the B15 bus to come (heading to church). While waiting, a man drove up in his SUV and got out. He walked up to me and began to share his testimony with me. He spoke of how good God had been to him, and how blessed he felt. Then he broke out in a shout! He looked at me afterwards and said, "praising God is what you must do, and do not be ashamed of the time or place that you do it." The man then returned to his car and went on his way.

I stood there for a moment reflecting on what the man said to me. When the bus finally came, I got on, sat down, and took my Bible out of my bag. I read the following scripture to myself:

### Psalm 34:1 (CEV)

"I will praise the Lord."

Right then as I was sitting on the bus, I began to praise God myself.

Every Saturday back in the day, we would gather at the house of the late Pastor G.E. Knight, to get ready to have church. She would say to me "Glory Hallelujah, thank you Jesus! Gilchrist, come on let us have church". While pointing her hand towards me, she would also say, "I do not know what you come here to do, but I am here to praise and bless the Lord!". Then she would ask me "Gilchrist are you here to praise and bless the Lord?" My answer of course was "yes, because he is worthy to be praised". We began to shout and dance and praise Him with all that we had! I love praising God and blessing His name. We carried on with our service and had a great time in the Lord.

I thank the Lord for this sermon that teaches us that being an onlooker in the arena of Christian living is taking a risk with your life. If we are to mature and grow stronger as followers of Jesus Christ, we need to venture out in faith and trust the process. You take a much greater risk if you do nothing more than become a spectator in your Christian walk. God calls us to get into the game, not to be a scorekeeper!

# ◇ 8 ◇

## Don't Be a Grumbler

*January 8, 2005*
*Saturday Night*

One Saturday morning (July 25,1978) when I was eight years old, I was doing my chores(cleaning the hallway) in my mother's home. While sweeping the floor, I heard my mother say that "God is good; we should not waste our time complaining too much". I playfully started using the broom handle as a microphone and began to preach.

I thank God for this sermon because it is true and helpful. It teaches us about not grumbling and complaining too much. We give many excuses and reasons why we complain – we are busy, bored, do not have enough money, underappreciated, do not like our church…etc. We could go on forever, finding things to complain about – but should we? Instead, try taking the time to look at and count your blessings. By the time you get through, you will have forgotten what you had to complain about in the first place.

"Do everything without grumbling or arguing".

**Philippians 2:14 (CEV)**

## 9

## Worship Only God

*May 4, 2006*
*Thursday Night*

This sermon makes us think about and examine who/what we are worshipping. Society has gotten to a point of carelessness with worshipping material things that we have. This can happen so quickly that you may not realize that you are doing it. We ought to be careful because anything can be made into an idol if you continually put it before God.

Nothing but God should be worshipped because nothing else can help you like He can. Do not worship your money, possessions, your homes, or even your jobs.

"Don't bow down and worship idols. I am the Lord your God, and I demand all your love. If you reject me, I will punish your families for three or four generations."

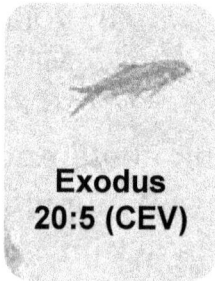

**Exodus 20:5 (CEV)**

## 10

## Music Feeds the Soul

*June 01, 2002*
*Saturday*

My godfather (the late Bishop Willie F. Jones, Jr.) picked me up and drove me to my godmother's (the late Pastor Gloria E. Knight) house. As we were driving, we listened to the gospel station WLIB 1190AM and praised God – letting the music soothe our souls. The music was so inspirational that I asked Bishop Jones to pull over for a minute because I felt a praise welling up inside of me. After he pulled over and parked, we both began to give God an intense praise and glory. That afternoon I preached a message that said "may our God give us a song today that will remind us of just how good and great he is - no matter what we may face.

## Expressing God's Love

*April 16, 1973*
*Sunday Night*

When I was a little boy, I discovered that some of our neighbors needed help. Sometimes they would come to our house and ask my mother if she could help them with what they needed, and she would always help them as much as she could.

She taught me that "if you see someone in need of help, do not ignore that person because you never know when you might find yourself in that same situation - and you would want someone to help you".

I thank God for this sermon that instructs us to allow our kind and gentle spirits to show others in need compassion, tolerance, understanding, and unconditional love. By doing this we express God's love through action.

"Treat others just as you want to be treated."

**Luke 6:31 (CEV)**

## We Are All Equal

The story behind this sermon comes from when I was a young boy and the lesson that my mother taught me about not acting like I was better than anyone else in this world. She stressed to me that just because someone else can do something better than me, that does not make them better than me. I do not remember my mother ever talking negative about anyone, or acting like she was better than anyone.

She would often say to me "Vincent, if anyone does anything bad/wrong to you, just pray for them and love them anyway". I would tell her that I could not pray for and be good to someone who mistreated me. Her reply was always the same –"Vincent, yes you can, because the love of Jesus in your heart will help you to do it!". I soon began to understand what she meant. I would say this prayer to myself "Dear Father, thank you for your love. Please help me to love others, like you love me. In Jesus name, Amen".

This sermon reminds me to share with others that it is not about you, me, or anyone else. People sadly think of themselves only sometimes, and this is a mistake. We must stop and think and do our best to use our talents for God, and to share with others.

I want to thank you Lord for giving me this sermon at an early age.

**Proverbs 30:13 (AMP)**

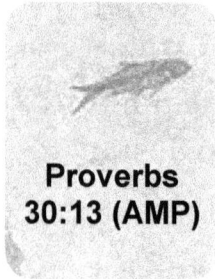

"There is a generation (class of people) – oh how lofty are their eyes! And their eyelids are raised in arrogance. Shame on you if you think you are better than anyone else. YOU ARE NOT."

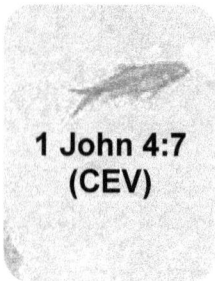

**1 John 4:7 (CEV)**

"My dear friends, we must love each other. Love comes from God, and when we love each other, it shows we have been given new life. We are now God's children, and we know him."

# ⟨13⟩

## Be the Light

January 01, 1989
Saturday

In my childhood my mother and I sang a song that I still sing today – "this little light of mine, I'm going to let it shine". Whenever I sing this song, I am singing about the light that comes from God, and how I want that light to shine brightly so everyone that is in my presence can see and feel it.

The world may be dark with sin, but Jesus gives light to the world. As Christians, He lives in us, so we must also give that light to the world. We are to be an example of love in this world and show/tell people that living for

Jesus is the best way to live. We must show others that our God **is** love and not let the world dim our light.

"You are the light for the whole world. A city built on top of a hill cannot be hidden, **15** and no one lights a lamp and puts it under a clay pot. Instead, it is placed on a lampstand, where it can give light to everyone in the house. **16** Make your light shine, so others will see the good you do and will praise your Father in heaven".

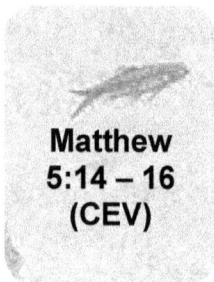

**Matthew 5:14 – 16 (CEV)**

## God, Your Father

*October 19, 1999*
*Saturday*

Have you accepted God as your Father? He loves you and wants to teach you how to improve your life. Will you let Him into your life, and allow Him to show you how? I was blessed to preach this sermon that God instructed me to give to His people about the importance of having Him in our lives. If we first allow Him in, and then allow Him to take over, we will see the change in ourselves for the better.

# 15

## Watch Your Mouth!

*January 17, 2004*
*Saturday*

This sermon is one that I have preached numerous times, and it has helped many people. From all walks of life, they tell me that not only has it helped them, but others that they shared it with, and it needs to be preached so that society can understand the danger of a loose tongue.

This sermon simply says that gossiping is a destroyer, and we should do our best to stay away from being a perpetrator of such a lifestyle. We must realize that we are not only hurting ourselves, but others as well. If you feel that you must say something that is not a positive or encouraging thing to talk about, then it is best left unsaid, or you can talk to Jesus about it. He will listen to you and then He will correct you where correction is needed.

We need to learn to lift each other up instead of putting each other down.

"You will say the wrong thing if you talk too much – so be sensible and watch what you say."

**Proverbs 10:19 (CEV)**

"Keep what you know to yourself, and you will be safe; talk too much, and you are done for."

**Proverbs 13:3 (CEV)**

◇ **16** ◇

## The Prayer Line

*March 7, 1979*
*Wednesday Night*

Forty-six years ago, when I was nine years old, God gave me a message to give to His people reassuring them that they can talk to Jesus any time of the day or night; He will always answer their prayers. This sermon was preached on a Wednesday night when my church (the Sacred Heart Church of Faith) had our weekly prayer meeting.

I requested of my Pastor (the late Bishop Edward L. Chamble) that he give me an opportunity to preach. He granted my request and I preached this message letting people know that Jesus is always available to them, to hear their prayers. But how can they call on Him if no one has ever told them about Him or they have not formed a relationship with Him? How can they believe in Him without hearing the message? Someone has to be willing to share that message with them – but, to preach the message, messengers must be sent. This was my message to the people, and after I finished preaching this Word, the people shared with me how blessed they felt through the sermon, and they encouraged me to keep spreading love with my preaching. I have not stopped preaching this sermon to this day because I know that it has an impact.

**Romans 10:14 – 15 (CEV)**

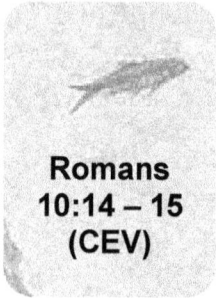

" 14 How can people have faith in the Lord and ask him to save them, if they have never heard about him? And how can they hear, unless someone tells them? 15 And how can anyone tell them without being sent by the Lord? The Scriptures say it is a beautiful sight to see even the feet of someone coming to preach the good news."

## Your Answer is Waiting

When I was a young boy there was a song that I loved singing in church called "Jesus is on the main line, tell Him what you want." One night I was watching television with my mother and a commercial came that said, "if you need a lawyer, call...", and it listed a phone number on the screen. I turned to my mother and said, "I know a good lawyer, His name is Jesus, and He will freely help you".

When you call an automated telephone system, they have instructions on which numbers to press to connect to someone that will help you get the kind of help that you need. I am glad that I do not have to go through all those steps to talk to Jesus when I need Him. He is always available for instant communication twenty-four hours a day and seven days a week. Access to Him is never denied.

When you have problems or troubles that you cannot handle, do not be afraid or worry. Just trust in Him and He will help you and bring you peace while you are waiting on Him.

# ⟨18⟩

## The Source of Joy

*April 3, 1990*
*Friday 1:00 AM*

I was in an all-night prayer meeting (at the Historic Washington Temple Church of God in Christ) praying at the altar. After finishing prayer, I took out a small pack of index cards that I had with me and began to write this sermon that the Lord gave to me.

This message lets us know that our joy comes from God. We have this joy because of His love for us and because we know that He truly cares for and about us. We have joy because we belong to Him. Praise God for the joy that He gives to us; no one can take away that joy! Praise God!

I had the opportunity to preach this sermon thirty-five years ago, at the age of twenty, at the Angelic Church of Signs and Wonders Miracle Church where the late Evangelist Gloria E. Knight was the Pastor – I was the Assistant Pastor at the time.

## ⟨19⟩

## Do Your Best

*August 29, 1993*
*Sunday 7:00 PM*

In life we may face situations that we do not like, or that we may not know how to handle. It becomes easy to complain/feel sorry for ourselves in these times, but instead of doing that, we must work hard and do our best to continue to serve God through those times. Jeremiah 29:11 (RSV) says, "For I know the plans I have for you, says the Lord, plans for welfare and not for evil, to give you a future and a hope".

I gave this sermon thirty-two years ago, at the age of twenty-five.

## Humility is Key

*February 5,2006*
*Sunday 5:00 PM*

This sermon that I was blessed to preach simply says to "be humble before God today". Examine your life, confess your sins, and ask for forgiveness (whether it be from others or from God). God will forgive you and help you to grow in Him. He will also help others to forgive you. After that you must forgive yourself!

## 21

## Be at Peace

*March 21, 1983*
*Sunday 5:00 PM*

I remember in my youth that above the door in the vestibule of my church (the Sacred Heart Church of Faith), there was a rectangular, white sign with a scripture in red letters –

### John 14:27 (CEV)

"I give you peace, the kind of peace only I can give. It isn't like the peace this world can give. So don't be worried or afraid."

I asked my pastor (the late Bishop Edward L. Chamble) if I could preach a sermon based on those words, and he agreed to allow me to do so.

My sermon said, "when bad times come, we do not need to be afraid or worry, we need only to trust Jesus; He will help us face all of our problems and give us peace". I thank God for the chance to preach this message, and for its encouraging and helpful theme.

It has been forty-two years since I first preached this sermon when I was thirteen years old. I will continue to preach this whenever God tells me to.

## Draw Nearer

*January 4, 2006*
*Wednesday 7:00 PM*

There is a song called "I Am Thine O Lord", that I love to sing. I thank God every day for that song; and this sermon reflects that both songs as well as teachings can lead you to decide if you want to be far away from God, or close to Him. God **wants** you to be near to Him, and to serve Him.

Trust God today to give you what you need - whatever that might be. Worship Him and enjoy serving Him. He will never let you down.

I preached this sermon nineteen years ago at the age of thirty-eight. It has blessed me many times over the years.

# Be A Witness

*February 20, 2009*
*Friday 3:00 PM*

One afternoon on my way to the pharmacy to get a prescription filled, as I was walking on Utica Avenue, heading towards St. John's Place, a young lady stopped me and asked me if I would mind praying for her – she wanted to give her life to the Lord. I told her that I would pray for her, and when I finished praying, and ministering to her, she gave her life to the Lord.

What a glorious, and victorious day for the Kingdom! I thank God for the opportunity not only to witness to the young lady, but also to be the catalyst that brought her to Him. This was sixteen years ago at the age of forty-two.

It is our job to be witnesses for Jesus. I hope that you get to be a witness to someone in need one day and share the good news about Him with someone that needs to know about His love and salvation.

I remember in 1985, the late, great Rev. Timothy Wright recorded an album that had the song "I'll Be a Witness" on it. I had an old cassette recorder, and I played this song so much that the tape broke. I made up my mind while listening to that song that being a witness for the Lord is what I wanted to do. Being a witness is important and rewarding.

I preached this sermon that night.

**Proverbs 11:30 (CEV)**

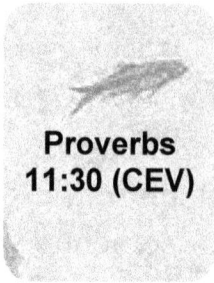

"Live right, and you will eat from the life-giving tree. And if you act wisely, others will follow."

**Matthew 4:19 (CEV)**

"Jesus said to them, "Follow me! I will teach you how to bring in people instead of fish.""

**Mark 16:20 (CEV)**

"Then the disciples left and preached everywhere. The Lord was with them, and the miracles they worked proved that their message was true."

# About the Author

Apostle Vincent J. Gilchrist is a native of Brooklyn N.Y. He is an anointed preacher, gospel singer, song writer, and author. He received his honorary Doctorate Degree of Divinity in November 2012. He believes in holiness and sanctification, and lives by the motto of **"*continually* pursue peace with everyone, and the sanctification without which no one will (ever) see the Lord."** (Hebrews 12:14 AMP).

His desire is to ensure that men, women, and children come to know Jesus as their Savior. He has been given a special gift and is known to be a great encourager to those in the Body of Christ. He preaches the Gospel with wisdom, simplicity, and love.

If you have never met or talked with Apostle Vincent J. Gilchrist; or if you are tired of the way things are in the world and you want to make a difference and make things better, then read this book. I know you will find some small tool within to help you.

www.ingramcontent.com/pod-product-compliance
Lightning Source LLC
Chambersburg PA
CBHW071025040426
42443CB00007B/936